RELATIONSHIPS

Patrick Broe

Copyright © 2017 by Patrick Broe
All rights reserved.

DEDICATION

This book is dedicated firstly to my wife, Peggy, she has been my partner on this journey and I could not have written this book without her. I cannot imagine life without her by my side.

Next, our boys William and Mark. There are no words to express the love and pride that they bring into my life. May this book be their legacy when I can no longer be with them.

To my brother and sisters, Eileen, Mary, Ann, Brendan, Joan, Maureen, Patricia, Philomena, Lorraine, Carol and Jane. Thank you for your love, acceptance and patience over the years.

I owe a huge debt to all of the people who have contributed in various ways to this book and the many amazing friends who carry us in their hearts. I apologise to anyone not mentioned, you know who you are and you have my humble thanks. Brian and Sharon, George and Christina, Kareen, Lily, Eve, Catherine, Roy, Ernie, Erica, Norman, Christine, Mairi, Margaret, Heide, Mary, Erica, Donella, Michael, Jack, Rhoda, Mark, Doleen, Angela, Jesse, Helen, Suzy, Ann, Ian, the wonderful girls from The Shed.

You are all inspirational, thank you for being you.

I must pay special tribute to the two people, no longer with us, without whom I simply would not be here. My father and mother, Patrick Bernard Broe and Mary Jane Broe.

CONTENTS

INTRODUCTION
DIGGING FOR TREASURE
RELATIONSHIPS R US

GROWING UP

ARRIVAL ON A STRANGE PLANET
WHAT IF?
FINDING A VOICE
RESCUE A CHILD
EVE'S GIFT
CHAOS, BALANCE, RIGIDITY

JOINING THE DOTS

SELF EXPRESSION
IS IT OKAY TO BE ME?
SHARED IDENTITY
A LADY NAMED GAGA

THROUGH THE FIRE

CHOOSE LIFE
BEAUTY
FINDING HOPE
HOPE
PAUL'S BIG SUCCESS
HOW ALCOHOL SAVED MY LIFE

RECOVERY
EULOGY
BETTER THAN WELL
MARK'S GIFT
MY GIFT
STARS
AWAKENING
ORDINARY PEOPLE

INTRODUCTION

This book has been a long time in the writing and has had many forms. Its journey reflects my own through life and I believe everyone else walks along a similar path.

I am a hairdresser and have been for over forty years. I have also studied and taught martial arts and various aspects of personal development. All of these roles have given me the opportunity to meet and work with people, up close and personal. I have seen again and again the crucial importance our relationships play in determining who we are and the ways that we experience our lives.

I want to remind you of who you really are, to help you decide what is truly important, indeed vital to your well-being. To shine a light on the treasures that are yours already or can be.

Our world is full of wonderful opportunities to connect, feel connected and expand our lives. There are no fees to pay and no exclusions, each and every one of us is born into this club.

I try to leave people that I have just met with two foundational gifts. I want then to feel that they are part of something bigger, not alone. I also want them to feel better about themselves than before we met. I call these foundational, because they mark the beginning of relationship.

It is not possible to cover every type of relationship in one book, nor even in one lifetime. However, I hope to demonstrate that all that we do, think or feel is relational by nature. If we can recognise this and relate to it, all of our relationships will be deeper, wider and more fulfilling.

We cannot survive and thrive in isolation, relationships really are us.

DIGGING FOR TREASURE

In the vastness of the universe it is extremely unlikely that life occurred once only, on our planet. We are tantalisingly close to finding evidence of life in one form or another, maybe even in our own solar system.

Out of billions of planets in millions of galaxies, across infinite space, the odds are that we are not alone.

However, it took four and a half billion years for us to arrive on our planet. We came into being from a series of huge biological changes, which were impossible to predict and far from guaranteed. The overwhelming majority of extra-terrestrial life is likely to be primitive. On the scale of the universe we are miniscule but in all probability very rare indeed.

If we are scarcer than gemstones or precious metals then shouldn't we value ourselves and each other more? If we found ourselves alone and isolated in space the thing we would miss most would be people.

As unlikely as this scenario might seem, there are times in our lives when we close ourselves off and block our connection to others. This is against our nature and shrinks our sense of self and self-worth.

We are surrounded by unique, valuable people, just like ourselves. They and we represent mines filled with life enhancing treasures waiting to be unearthed but to find them we have to dig.

RELATIONSHIPS R US

I have always been interested in people and what makes us tick. I read and studied many books and ideas on the subject of us but I'd never thought of building my own ideas into a working formula.

That changed one night when I discovered that a young schoolgirl, who worked for me on Saturdays, had tried to commit suicide.

It turned out that she was being bullied at school and seeing no way out, took this desperate step.

When I spoke to her I explained that she had a choice to make. If she wanted the bullies to win then she could continue to think that she was useless and worthless, in which case, she shouldn't bother to return to work. However, if she believed that she was worth fighting for and deserved a chance to prove them wrong, then she should be back the next Saturday.

She arrived bright and early for work and Relationships R Us was born.

It began as a workplace training programme for all of our staff but evolved into a blueprint for life.

We started with "why this job as opposed to something else?". If the answer was "we hadn't got the grades to do something better" then I would suggest go work somewhere else. You deserve to have a successful rewarding career and your clients deserve great service from you. The one unique thing that you bring to any job is you. The only thing you ever really have to offer is you and clients can only get that from you.

Life is short and work takes up a lot of that time, so find a career that you can have a long rewarding relationship with and keep looking till you do.

Apart from the practical skills needed to do our job we need to be good with people. We should want to know them, want to please them and build relationships with them so that they keep coming back.

In order to relate to others we must be able to relate to ourselves. If we want to be happy, we must accept ourselves feel comfortable in our own skin.

Maintaining successful relationships with other people is one of the most important ways we assess ourselves. It allows us to connect with others and feel connected. We need to value ourselves to be able to value anyone else, which in turn makes us feel valued by others.

At first the thought of building relationships, when you feel that you have little to give and so much to learn is scary. We began with the good relationships that we already had - family, friends, teachers, etc.

These people got something from spending time with us and we benefitted from connecting with them. We didn't have to reinvent the wheel; we already were hard wired to connect with other people.

We discussed the fact that we and everybody else play contrasting roles or act differently depending on who we are with. These are all aspects of who we are, indeed the role must be authentically you, or the other person will sense a lack of depth and lose interest or trust.

Looking at other people's behaviour helped us to see similarities in ourselves.

We noted that some needed rigidity, rules and regulation in their lives. When we examined this trait in ourselves, it usually accompanied feelings of insecurity or fear of losing control.

Sensing the ways in which our feelings and emotions affected our mood helped us to empathise with others and gradually to realise that the world around us doesn't change much, but our perception of it does.

Once we understood that feelings are thoughts, we grasped that we could change our thoughts and those of others to improve the way we all feel.

This discovery was momentous; our young lady learned that acceptance of herself, without judgement, allowed her to accept everybody, without judging them. Acceptance is the first step to building a relationship. Even when we can't heal another person or fix their problem, we can make them feel connected, felt and accepted.

She had been rejected, not accepted, by the bullies but she learned to accept herself and reject the thought that she was worthless. At this point we began to explore what we really wanted, if we were prepared to commit and work hard, what would success look like?

To help find answers to this we listened to the theme song from the movie, 'Flashdance'. I had found the lyrics inspirational when I was younger, training hard for martial arts.

We discussed the central theme of finding something that would ignite our passion and become a vehicle to focus and develop us into becoming the person we wanted to be.

Every client was an opportunity to perform and fine tune our skills, practical and interpersonal. It became clear that the better we connected with other people our own experience was deeper and more rewarding. We accepted that hairdressing may not always give us the scope for growth that we needed but at that point it ticked all the boxes.

One afternoon per week was set aside to develop the program and if anything came up that couldn't wait, we discussed it. A number of tools were employed to keep the message fresh, including the flea story and the word indispensable.

If you have ever seen a flea circus it appears amazing, how do they train fleas to perform tricks? The truth is fleas can't learn tricks but fleas can jump, some species can jump fifty times their own body length. The trick requires the flea to jump a specific distance so the flea is placed in a container with a lid at exactly the height needed. The flea tries to leap out to freedom but repeatedly hits it's head on the lid.

Even fleas don't like sore heads but they have no choice but to jump. Eventually they learn to leap to just below the lid height and once that happens, they never jump higher. Human beings do this to themselves all the time. They decide that they can go so far and no further, without even trying.

We call this a glass ceiling.

Most of the time people use the word indispensable, as a negative, "no one is indispensable". However we can look at it in other ways. Neither my wife nor I are indispensable to the institution of marriage but we are both indispensable to our marriage.

We can also break the word down into three smaller words: In, Dispense and Able.

If we think of *In* as part of something dynamic and growing, from time to time problems get in the way and we need to *Dispense* with these issues to be *Able* to move on. This is a regular process, not a once in a lifetime event.

Over several years we developed the program alongside practical skills and targeted career development training. We were thrilled to be nominated for and win a National Training Award – a huge recognition of how far we all had come.

At the Awards dinner, I was overcome to see our confident, beaming young lady talking to one of British industry's leading lights. He was congratulating her on what she had achieved and asking what she might do next.

At the time of writing this, some years later, I am proud to say that she has gone on to run her own successful business and is currently a very happy wife and mother.

GROWING UP

ARRIVAL ON A STRANGE PLANET

None of us can remember our own birth, or arrival on a strange planet. We begin our lives completely helpless, reliant on others for our very survival. Luckily the vast majority of new parents are hard wired to love and nurture, they embark on a lifelong commitment to their precious new baby.

I vividly remember that moment with William, our oldest son. It had been a long and painful labour for my wife after more than 36 hours and an emergency caesarean section, William arrived. I returned to the maternity ward with William and a nurse, dazed and worrying about my wife, still in the operating theatre.

William softly whimpered and I slid my hand into the incubator to touch and soothe him. He reached up and wrapped his tiny hand around my little fingernail.

I was overwhelmed by emotions, nothing before prepared me for that blinding moment of undiluted love. Tears streamed down my face, I was dumbstruck by the connection between us. I knew from that moment on, this beautiful boy would be part of me. A truly life changing experience.

Although as babies can do very little for ourselves, we use all the tools at our disposal to establish, build and develop a relationship with our parents.

These aliens soon teach us that we are connected to them and indeed the rest of mankind.

Before we can do almost anything else, we start to build relationships because our survival depends on it. This need for connection to others is with us all of our lives.

FINDING A VOICE

I was fortunate, I had loving parents. My parents were also Catholic, though not regular church goers, they believed in God. Children believe what their parents tell them and we were taught about a loving father, who would forgive us, provided that there was no malice intended and we were genuinely penitent. We were encouraged to seek a relationship with God.

One day at my Catholic school when I was about seven years of age, a nun, teaching the class informed us that in time we would die and if we did not behave and think as she instructed, we would go to hell to be punished. If this was intended to scare us into compliance, it failed miserably, in my case at least.

I spent several days trying to think of places to die where God could not find me, distant planets, undersea caves and the like. However, I concluded that if God made everywhere, then there was nowhere he couldn't find me. So I decided to confront God, where was his love and forgiveness?

This wasn't the God that I knew from my home life and I couldn't believe that my parents would leave me to the whims of an unjust, vengeful God. I eventually reasoned that God was loving and understanding but that the nun and others were misrepresenting God for their own purposes.

What we believe has a direct and powerful effect on the way we live our lives. We make assumptions based on what we believe and if the world we make for ourselves doesn't work for us, we find it very difficult to let go of those beliefs.

We all have an inner voice, usually sensed rather than heard. It carries on a narrative throughout our lives, sometimes suggesting or judging or just observing. Each of us assigns a level of importance or even a persona to the voice. After all, we can't just ignore it.

At that time, I believed that my voice was God in direct relationship with me; it would be some time before I recognised the true nature of the voice.

WHAT IF?

As children, we have an amazing ability to invent and reinvent ourselves.

We can be pirates, cowboys or Indians anything that we choose. We are able to give ourselves to the role, unselfconsciously and expect our playmates to abide by the rules of the game. These flights of fancy can seem very real when we are young and our brains are developing.

I remember walking to school trying desperately not to step on the cracks in the pavement; there would be terrible consequences if I did. Like a lot of children, my friends and I would sometimes pretend to be invisible. We would take specific routes home, sprinting between invisibility corridors.

We loved simply being children, if we thought about adulthood, we assumed that there was a certain age at which we changed - stopped being children and became serious, knowledgeable and adult. Although we never discussed it we thought that adulthood was a clearly defined role that you acquired, off the peg and simply put on.

As time went on and nobody stepped forward to give us this new persona, we began to worry. Could we be expected to find this for ourselves? We didn't know where to look, eventually we created roles to try but we worried that these wouldn't be good enough. Our quest for approval led us into a period of insecurity, self criticism and doubt. Some of us struggle with these feelings throughout our lives.

The truth is there is no off the peg model for an adult and we are capable of changing who we are, into who we want to be - all of our lives. We just need to be brave enough to think, what if?

RESCUE A CHILD

I have spoken to many people over the years, who have been traumatised by something, whilst still children. These can be singular events or persistent and continuing throughout childhood.

Children need their relationships with adults to be honest and trustworthy. The adult is always expected to take the lead and guide the child, when this trust is broken, even unintentionally, it throws our understanding of our world into chaos.

We can neither make sense of the way we feel nor understand how someone we felt so connected to becomes a stranger.

We long for reassurance that everything will be alright. Sadly if our home life is afflicted by addiction and or abuse, this is unlikely to happen. We feel frightened, isolated and terribly alone.

I have listened as victims, now parents or even grandparents themselves, relive their terrifying childhood experiences and are reduced to lost, lonely children in desperate need of rescue.

In order for us to experience peace, without judgement, we must connect with, accept and develop a relationship with our inner child. For our own sake, we must return to that damaged child within, take their hand, calm their fear and convince them that they have been heard. We are united and will complete life's journey together.

Forgive the past and free the future.

If we can see our world as a child, with wonder, forgiveness and endless possibilities, then the child within us rescues us.

As I mentioned not all such relationships are damaged intentionally. When I was 14 years old my father died, he did not die intentionally but his loss felt almost like betrayal, abandonment.

I struggled to cope with life without him. He was security and protection, not just for me but all of my family. I have ten sisters and one brother. I was the younger boy but my older brother was married, living away from home. I was swamped with feelings that I must somehow replace my father give that security and protection to my mother and sisters. I was overwhelmed by the avalanche of things that I would not be able to deal with, then, one night, I had a dream.

In the dream I woke up in my parents' bedroom, we lived in a three storey Victorian townhouse with a coal cellar in the basement. My parents' room was on the first floor at the top of the stairs. There was a loud banging from downstairs. I felt nervous but as the new man of the house knew that I had to investigate the noise.

Slowly with my back to the wall, I made my way down the stairs. To my horror, when I reached the hallway, the noise was still coming from below. The cellar was a place of dread to us as children, even aged fourteen the idea of going down there alone, at night, filled me with fright.

I knew that I had to protect my family and so must go down into the cellar. I had never felt so alone before or since. Each downward step made my heart beat faster and faster, my eyes and ears were straining to reveal what monster waited for me in the dark. Finally I reached the floor below and turned into the coal cellar.

I couldn't believe my eyes, in the middle of the room stood the devil himself. Terror raced through me, I couldn't move. How could I, a teenage boy, possibly deal with this but my family had to be protected.

I had to try to fight, I had become involved with the martial arts when I was eleven years old and all I could think to do was try to fight the devil with what I knew. At first he moved too quickly and then when I did manage to hit him, it hurt me rather than him but then something amazing happened!

Just as I thought I had run out of options and knew that I couldn't win, in my mind's eye I could see crucifixes appear across my knuckles and on the soles of my feet. The next time I landed a blow, it sent him flying across the room. My confidence soared and I kicked and punched the devil around the cellar, he moaned with pain and eventually staggered and lurched his way up the steps. I raced after him, he fumbled with the back door handle and half fell into the back yard. Once there he hauled himself over the garden wall and ran away into the night. I watched from the doorway leaping and cheering with my arms in the air.

At that moment, I knew that I could not win every battle that I would meet but that for the rest of my life, I would never be alone.

Aged fourteen, I believed that God had saved me.

The idea of life without my father to guide and protect me left me crushed by grief and a terrible sense of responsibility to try to fill his shoes. My dream showed me that even when faced with the seemingly impossible, you can find the resources to survive.

The boy who looked everywhere for connection and relationship rescued me.

EVE'S GIFT

It is all too easy to confuse what we think or feel with reality.

When my son was about four years old he picked up a virus and for the first time that he can remember, he vomited. Frightened and confused, throwing up and crying at the same time, he couldn't breathe properly. This was so traumatic for him that for many years, every time he got excited or breathless from running or stressed at all, he suffered a panic attack.

Long after he had forgotten the original experience, a word, a smell or anything at all that he had learned to associate with those feelings, would trigger a spiral of terrifying thoughts and physical sensations.

It was awful, as parents, to see your child in such distress and feel so helpless. There was no monster to chase away and no reassurance we could give. The danger came from within his own mind.

If he was trapped and alone inside his thoughts, then we had to find a way to reach him, be with him and help him to see his fear for what it was. Over time and with help, we helped him to understand his feelings, to manage and eventually stop the panic attacks.

Feelings and emotions are thoughts, they are not reality. If we can take a breath and step back, we often see a bigger picture. No matter how much we want to run from or change reality, we can't, but there is always something that we can do to make it better.

I know an exceptional young lady named Eve, who understands this very well.

For pretty much all of Eve's life, she is fourteen, her father has been fighting cancer. Her family are amazing people who understand that life is for living, whether short or long. Their love for each other and concern for others are inspirational.

Eve had been growing her hair for a special purpose, she wanted it to reach waist length then she would cut it and donate it to make wigs for cancer patients. Despite being several inches from her target, she recently decided that today is the day.

Her father had just started another round of aggressive treatments and had lost his hair. Eve told me that it was time. "Dad doesn't have a choice about losing his. I have long, luxurious hair and I see girls so concerned with their hair and the way it looks and it just seems so unimportant".

I am immensely proud of Eve, at a time when others might think only of themselves and ask why me, she finds a place in her heart to think of others. While there is still an Eve in our world then we have the gift of hope.

CHAOS, BALANCE, RIGIDITY

When our relationships with ourselves and the world around us are in balance, we feel energised and alive. If we're drawn towards either chaos or rigidity, we feel out of control and isolated. We cannot relate to anyone or anything. For relationship engines, which we are, this shuts us down. We lose our sense of self.

Events that threaten us can trigger a fight, flight or freeze response. Sometimes this feels so real that we can become trapped in a cycle of chaotic or rigid behaviour.

We need to be able to link the threat to our response and recognise that our feelings of dread, fear and helplessness are thoughts, generated by our own mind.

This is what happened with my son's panic attacks. In his mind all of the details of the original event, the physical sensations, the sounds, smells everything became triggers for panic and every subsequent attack brought fresh triggers. He needed to find a safe place for his consciousness to be, whilst the triggers emerged - being able to observe these feelings and fears, but not be swept away by them.

As there was no present threat, over time the feelings simply dissolved. He was gradually freed from the rigid rituals, once employed to protect him and the chaos of feeling totally out of control. The tools that allowed him to withdraw from his feelings and see a different reality restored his sense of balance.

JOINING THE DOTS

SELF EXPRESSION

I first became interested in the martial arts at the age of eleven. My best friend Mark and I attended classes at a local Chinese Kung Fu school. We had learned a little Judo and wanted to try something new. We were dedicated students, training hard seven nights a week. We were keen to learn the philosophy as well as the Kung Fu. At that point we believed in systems, we felt that the right formula would transform us into who and what we wanted to be.

Sadly, we had no idea who we wanted to be.

We worked hard to be good at this and to achieve that but without a real sense of purpose. We were like puppets dancing to someone else's tune. We enjoyed the physical challenge of the training and we were good at it, but it felt as if something was missing. We didn't know what was missing until Bruce Lee lit up our world like a supernova. He cut the puppet strings and set us free.

Watching him move, hearing his words and reading his ideas opened up a whole new world. He was the complete package, he knew who he was, what he wanted and what he needed to do to get it. He taught us that systems produce systematic responses.

The only way to find and free yourself was to have no system; to take whatever worked and use it without prejudice or prejudgement.

We set about changing our martial art to fit us. We cut away everything that was not essential. Those essential elements were practiced until they became part of us. For the first time in our lives we became the project, we worked on every aspect of our selves in order to become who we wanted to be.

This was not restricted to martial arts training sessions; it touched every part of our lives. We became more connected, confident, balanced and happier because of our relationships with martial arts and each other.

Although we had abandoned systems our new art needed a name, we called it Self Expression because that is what it became. We learned to be and express who we most wanted to be. The authentic me that we all want to celebrate.

IS IT OKAY TO BE ME?

I have always enjoyed helping others to recognise their potential and start them on the road to realising it.

For some this happened through martial arts training. Usually they would start out feeling awkward and a little nervous, wanting to prove something to themselves and win the respect of others.

As our art is about Self Expression the training is focussed on personal development. Over time they learn to relax, be themselves and make the most of their talents. Not everyone can be Bruce Lee but we can all achieve greater success when we stop worrying about failing.

For a while I was involved in management skills courses, now better known as team leadership courses. The title leads some to mistakenly believe that they will be trained to become leaders. The real purpose of such courses is to help to establish your natural role in the make up of a team, in addition to studying team dynamics and what makes a team perform well.

One such course was for a group of English public school students. They already had clearly defined roles and relationships as they had attended and boarded at the same schools for years.

We mixed them up in to slightly less familiar teams. Our course was made up of many outdoor pursuits and problems to be solved. Throughout we used a paper psychometric testing programme to explore and reveal the characteristics and traits of each student. The individual scores, results and conclusions were confidential, shared only with the student, not the school.

The main point was to help the students better understand how they naturally fitted into teams or groups, making the best use of their own abilities and getting the most out of the team. During the final individual briefings, we were delighted that two students had transformed their status by becoming team leaders. Two more who began the course afraid to speak up for themselves, went home brimming with confidence and a real sense of belonging to their group.

When we feel that we can never measure up to what others expect, we need to take another look, realise that we all have a place and a part to play. It is always okay to be me.

SHARED IDENTITY

Success quite often requires collaboration with other people. This can be in business or community projects, or even individual pursuits, such as achieving success in sport. We need to bring others with us on the journey, even an actor needs an audience. These relationships enrich, inform and enable the project.

First comes a purpose. A business needs a product or market, a project needs a need to fill and a sporting challenge must have a defined goal.

Next, we need resources to achieve our objective. Some of these will be human resources. Once in place, our resources must be managed, in line with our plan for success.

Attracting the right people to help build this success both as contributors and consumers or supporters is easier to do if you have recognisable values and principles. They give you an identity. This identity is your way of expressing to others and to yourself, what to expect from you. This is not merely a name above the door: your identity is ingrained in your project as in a stick of rock candy.

If you want to attract large numbers of people to work with you or support you then you must be flexible, accept and respect the needs and points of view of others. At the same time, you must try to remain true to your core values which make up your identity.

There will be times when you fail to live up to this image, for a variety of reasons but if you persevere, you will succeed.

In life, we are the project we will spend our entire lives working on. We are always in the process of becoming, it never ceases.

Our identity is that which we most want to be, it grows, evolves and changes but the values that underpin it are essentially us. This is common to each one of us and gives us a shared identity.

A LADY NAMED GAGA

I cannot write about relationships without paying tribute to an extraordinary woman. Without her I simply would not have my family, she was my mother in law Catherine.

For the first two years of our courtship I never met my future wife's mother. I had a Catholic background and in a predominately Presbyterian community, this was frowned on to say the least. My partner, Peggy, suffered a lot of abuse from several members of her church. Some even told her that her deceased father would be ashamed of her and might even disown her.

I have always believed in giving people a chance, prejudice of any kind blinds us to the humanity we share. Eventually I got to meet Catherine, she was ill and I helped Peggy to look after her. During this time, she started to see me, rather than the heathen Catholic!

We found that we had a lot in common. Although Catherine had missed several years in school because of a misdiagnosed back problem, she was interested in everything and read as much as she could.

We had many wonderful conversations covering a wide spectrum of topics, even religion. She was always gracious enough to admit if she was wrong and more than delighted to point out my errors. Over time our respect for one another grew until we learned to love each other. When Peggy and I were married, she was bursting with joy and pride.

She was a proud woman and fiercely independent, never asking for help if she could do it herself. One day she asked me to turn the mattress on her bed as it was becoming uncomfortable. When I saw the old bed, I couldn't believe that she got any sleep. The mattress had long since collapsed with springs sticking out of it. I couldn't bear the thought of her spending one more night in it, the next day I bought her a new bed.

Catherine was overcome, she was thrilled with her new bed but failed to see why she was worth all the bother. For me, it was the best money I had ever spent.

When our eldest son was born, she was happier than I had ever seen her. Having lost a child during pregnancy years before, this finally was her boy. Catherine doted on William, named after her husband, and William adored his Gaga. He couldn't manage to say granny at that time.
To watch them play together would brighten the darkest of days. Four years later our second child Mark arrived and Gaga's world was complete. She had everything she could wish for. She never really forgave herself for her initial hostility to our relationship but she knew that we did.

For two more years she filled our lives with love, she embraced life with the wonder and excitement of a child, unable to quite believe how blessed she was.

One night while talking on the phone, she suffered a stroke. Peggy and I were there in minutes and got her to hospital. We were told that there was no chance of a recovery and that she would not regain consciousness.

On the long walk home that night, Peggy and I prayed that we might get the chance to tell her we loved her and say goodbye.

Although Catherine seemed to be in a deep coma, we talked and read to her, told her stories. One of her favourites was a story that was told to the children in church on the day that Mark, our youngest son, was baptised.

The minister told them of a boy long ago who longed to grow up and become a shepherd, like his father. One Sunday, his minister explained that the lord was a shepherd. Indeed, he told them to count on their fingers beginning with the thumb, the words "The Lord is MY shepherd".

Hold on to that fourth finger he said, the word MY means that the lord is your personal shepherd. The young boy loved that idea. Months later on a snowy winter night, the boy's father was ill in bed and couldn't bring the sheep in from the hills. The young man was thrilled to take on the task, a shepherd at last.

Whilst gathering the sheep he fell from a steep hilltop breaking a leg. He was stuck unable to move and alone. With no hope of rescue, he curled into a ball and held his fourth finger, repeating over and over, "The lord is MY shepherd".

After a while his parents became worried, they raised all of the men of the village to search for their boy. Finally, he was found, covered with snow and apparently unconscious. As he was lifted and carried home the men heard him mumbling the words "the Lord is MY shepherd".

I told and retold this story to Gaga as she lay there, not knowing if she heard. After three days she woke up, she could do very little and was unable to speak. Catherine lived for three more weeks, during that time we got to care for her, surround her with our love and eventually say goodbye. It was a very special time.

One afternoon I asked her if she had been able to hear us while she was asleep, she held up her fourth finger and held on to it with the fingers of the other hand.

THROUGH THE FIRE

CHOOSE LIFE

I have spent my whole career starting and building relationships, with colleagues and clients.

Thirty years ago, I moved to an island in the Outer Hebrides, met my wife and settled down.

A lot of my clients have stayed with me all of that time. I have seen families grow up, go away to university, return home, marry and raise children of their own. Some have dealt with illness and loss, some have died. Everyone has their personal story and I have been privileged to have been a part of many, many stories.

Sometimes people find it possible to talk to their hairdresser when they can't find a way to speak to anyone else. I have always encouraged this, at times we all need a shoulder to cry on or just someone to listen. These moments have always been special and will remain confidential.

I never thought that I would need a shoulder and when it happened, I had to fall apart completely before I found it in me to ask for help.

My wife and I had been very happily married for nearly twenty years when she began to have a serious problem with alcohol. Up till then we had been real partners in everything we did, caring for our boys, running a business, just being together.

For a while, I didn't notice, alcoholics are very good at covering their tracks. Eventually I started to notice little things, on Sunday mornings she abandoned the usual lie in and got up early to drink.

I discovered wine in her teacup.

At first, I believed it was a minor problem. We were so close, we could handle anything. Over time our lives spun more and more out of control. She was our Company Secretary, responsible for paying accounts. Our business and personal financial situation became chaotic. We drifted further apart every day, to me it felt as if she was having an affair with alcohol. Our home life became a war zone, our boys' once happy parents became monsters.

Relationships were my thing, I prided myself on being able to help heal damaged relationships. However, the most important relationships in my life were collapsing around me and I couldn't stop or fix it. This went on for several years. I regained control of our finances but our marriage continued to break down. We said and did some awful things to each other. Eventually, one night, I'd had enough.

I went out for a walk, I didn't really know where I was going but I knew that I wasn't coming back.

I found myself facing the sea. I could see myself walking into the water, it looked and felt like the best thing I could do. I didn't particularly want to die, I just wanted peace.

At that moment, a boy rescued me.

I pictured my youngest son, Mark's face. All of the emotions bottled up inside me seemed to explode. Everything that I'd tried to contain and control flowed out of me. It was like a release of electricity and when I recovered awareness, I knew that everything was different.

I felt ashamed and renewed, no matter how bad I felt things were for me, that boy did not deserve to lose his father. I remembered the betrayal that I felt when my own father died, and that wasn't his choice. I could not do that to my sons.

I knew that I must let go of my wife, perhaps the reality of losing everything might bring her to her senses. My responsibility and only chance of survival was to try to recover myself and the boys, show them, myself and their mother that life is worth fighting for.

When I returned home, I wrote the most difficult email that I have ever written, to a very good and close friend. I cried for help and he came running, something for which I will always be profoundly grateful.

In the end, my need for connection and relationship was so strong it saved my life.

BEAUTY

I wrote Beauty at the time I separated from Peggy. I was overwhelmed by what was happening but wanted to document my feelings. I also wanted her to have them, to remind her of who she was.

BEAUTY

I cannot let you go without a final word which I hope will help you on your journey but regardless, it needs to find expression from deep within me.

First, I must pay tribute to the beautiful soul I once knew. She was beautiful by any and all measure, shone beauty through appearance and far more through simply being. For a spell we walked together and saw the beauty of all life around us, the pure magic that other people bring to our lives. I think we even put a little beauty and magic back into the world around us.

Greatest of all we brought new life of incalculable beauty and most of all love into this world. That was a privilege that I will carry with me always.

Love and beauty have their price, my beautiful soulmate is no more accessible to me. She is lost somewhere inside herself, consumed by a need not to look on herself. She desperately needs love, mostly from herself but cannot or will not allow herself to feel it, express it or simply live it.

I can no longer be by her side and watch and wait for her return. The love for our boys and life itself, compel me to walk a different path. I long with all I can find left of the memory of my beautiful soulmate that she can find her way back to the vital, authentic person lost within.

Hopefully the pride her sons have in her for being brave

enough to try will be a beacon in the dark for her and help to lead her home. For us, our days of sunlight in the garden are over, but she can still rebuild that strongest of bonds that connects her to the awesome lives she brought into this beautiful world.

FINDING HOPE

This will be difficult for my wife to read as it is hard for me to write.

I began the difficult but necessary process of separating from my wife, moved into a single bedroom and spoke to solicitors about divorce. I tried to convince her that she should leave the family home but she had nowhere to go. We tried to find a way of living under the same roof but the bitterness and all-consuming relationship with alcohol made it impossible.

I was shocked at what I had almost done and terrified that I might reach that point again. Following advice and in desperation, I called the police to remove her from our home. This started an unexpected and humiliating process ending in court. At this time, a police officer informed me that I was a victim. I found that label very hard to bear.

It felt like my life was in ruins but I had to do everything that I could to save my sons and myself from this nightmare. Once I began speaking about our situation to people friends, family and clients, it turned out that it was common knowledge, an open secret.

At first, I found talking about our lives painful and difficult, but it became easier as I discovered more and more people with similar and heart-breaking stories. Children growing up with two alcoholic parents, in utter chaos and total absence of love or care. Others like our children, with one parent suffering from alcoholism and the other not knowing how to cope. One explained how she watched her mother die. Still more were living in shattered marriages and some who could take no more and tried to move on with their lives.

It is easy to see the damage that drugs and alcohol do to the addicts but the children, partners, family and friends are too often forgotten and don't feel that they have a voice. It felt to me like a black hole sucking in all of my resources, financial, emotional, physical, mental and devouring them until all that was left was an empty husk, a shadow of a person.

In this game, everyone is a victim but we don't have to let that label define us forever.

Eventually and with no real hope of saving her marriage but maybe her relationship with her children, my wife decided to try to save herself. This took enormous courage and unbelievable determination.

We were both on different journeys but both supported by amazing people. No matter what your circumstances, if you are brave and humble enough to seek help. You can find love, support and understanding in what I now call the community of healing and recovery.

Trials test relationships and the outcomes are not always predictable. In our case, some of the people that we believed we could rely on disappeared. Others surprised us completely with their friendship and generosity.

Sometimes when we let go of something precious, we find something priceless.

A year after the boy rescued me from the sea I found a way to reach out to my best friend.

My now sober wife, Peggy and I began a new, stronger, better relationship, founded on the reality of who we are, not who we want each other to be. We are filled with hope as we join our many friends on the road to recovery.

HOPE

This was written for our sons, during our separation.

HOPE

Hope is finding reasons to believe. Believing gives you a framework and direction for your life.

YOU are both the reason hope exists and why it exists.

Today I feel less depressed because I have found a reason to hope.

Our happiness doesn't depend on other people but our sadness can.

We often try to present ourselves to the world in ways designed to win its approval, we want to be loved by others. We try to be what we think they want, but ultimately that makes us unhappy.

We can't make other people happy, we can't give them hope or give their lives purpose. We can only do that for ourselves.

Mum's problem has been dragging us all down because it makes each one of us powerless.

It takes away all hope of things getting better and breaks apart our ideal framework and sense of direction for our lives.

We reach a point where we can't find mum anymore she is lost in a place without hope and we can't even communicate with her because she has to hide even from herself.

We feel that our only way forward is to free ourselves from this destructive force.

We feel confused and angry because someone we used to rely on for so much has turned on us and now represents nothing but lies, unreliability and a terrible need that we can't possibly fulfil.

Our only healthy way forward is to find hope in ourselves.

I still have my framework and direction for my life. I need to revisit that, remember why I chose that and remember to love myself. We all need that.

You are loved deeply and unreservedly by your parents and that's great but you need to love yourself. Have hope and belief in yourself because you're your own best friend.

At the moment, your mother wants to try to make up for her behaviour by trying to be what she thinks each of us wants her to be but that will fail for sure.

Firstly, because the level of proof that we would need to be able to trust her with our emotions again is unattainable.

Secondly, and probably more importantly, she is trying to make someone else happy when she is not - that cannot work.

I believe the only way forward for her and us is to find hope for herself, to learn again how to love and like herself.

To remember and reinvent who she is everyday so that life and all its possibilities are exciting and open to her and each one of us.

This world can be a wonderful place of discovery and fulfilment if we allow ourselves to experience it and engage with it.

For my part, I'm sorry that my anger took over for a while. I think I'm naturally a hopeful and optimistic person.

I will do my best to live by what I have said and to help you to love, live and grow into who you will spend your entire life becoming.

PAUL'S BIG SUCCESS

This was written in gratitude to a police officer. He helped me enormously, by giving me a different perspective on my situation.

Thanks again Paul.

PAULS' BIG SUCCESS

Sometimes caring enough to try to help a person deal with trauma in their lives is just the reminder they need to deal with it themselves - put it into context and move on.

Paul did that for me and I'd like to thank him for waking me up. His obvious care and patience, allowed me to tell my story and his, again obvious conclusion, that I had become a victim of alcoholism, without being the alcoholic.

For a while that bothered me, I pride myself on helping other people with their problems and have always believed that I would put myself in harms way to protect others. The label victim didn't sit well with me. Until I realised that, without really understanding what I was doing, I was volunteering to take on the fight with alcohol on my partner's behalf. I would take anything that it could throw at me in order to save my partner.

I made some bad decisions and sacrificed a lot, pointlessly as it turns out.

There are times when we can protect and help people who are unable, for whatever reason, to do it for themselves. However, there are battles that we must fight for ourselves and win or lose our commitment to the fight defines who we are in the most important court in this world, our own mind. If we give it our all, no matter the personal cost, we will have earned self respect, a prize beyond value.

I urge anyone feeling lost or powerless to find a way back to the person inside, give that person respect and a proper place in the world. It will open up the possibility of a new and richer life.

HOW ALCOHOL SAVED MY LIFE

Written during our period of separation and when we were moving apart.

HOW ALCOHOL SAVED MY LIFE

For quite some time now I have been a victim of someone else's problem with alcohol.

I unwittingly chose to do that. I believed that the bonds between us were so strong and secure that I could save my partner and together we could be free of this destructive, all-consuming relationship. I, without realising the consequences for my family or myself, dived in without a thought, to someone else's personal hell.

Once there I struggled to find my partner, for a while I believed that I had, but in that uncharted, unfamiliar ocean, I was lost. I kept calling out to her and listening for her response but every time I thought she was close by it turned out to be just another mermaid, looking so much like my partner but trying to lead me only to her home in the murky deep.

Sometimes I would find her and think she was waving for me to come and save her, only to find as I came close, that she was drowning, not waving. There were times when I managed to grab hold of her and tried to keep her afloat, alas this was her ocean not mine, and I couldn't keep her head above the waves for long. I felt so helpless and useless and believed that I saw blame in her eyes that I couldn't save her.

Recently, I heard that I had become a victim on this dark water which was not my own. I wondered if I should accept that and simply stop swimming. Then it occurred to me that I had been swimming and that this was not my ocean. I couldn't find my bearings in the water but maybe, if I made landfall, it would give me a new perspective.

Once on solid ground, I found that I had been mistaken. I had never found nor had hold of my partner on that foreign ocean. When I thought I had found her and tried to pull her free, it was myself I was trying to waken, my very soul cried out SAVE ME.

I have learned to fear other people's oceans for my place is just not there. It is so easy to become lost and so alone. I hope that my old friend can find her own way to her shore, from there it's a wonderful view.

For me, I have finally managed to rescue myself and intend to live life as if brand new.

There is much that I find that has been salvaged and after the flood, with hope and with love, I can allow myself to live and grow and laugh and cry, enjoying this brief existence in all of its beauty and wonder.

EULOGY

At the time this was written I believed that Peggy would not survive.

It speaks for itself.

EULOGY

It is hard to know where to begin when you want to celebrate the life of someone special, you have loved and lost.

I guess a big part of our legacy is the impact we have on other people.

For me, she changed the direction and focus of my life.

She made me want to put down roots and plant the seeds of a new life together.

We started a business, made friends, created a family and filled our time with love and plans for the future.

She was bright, funny, beautiful and always left a void when she wasn't there.

She was amazing at all the things she did.

A fabulous mother

Supportive wife

Committed worker

The very best of friends

A truly unique person who exuded love and a joy for life

She made you feel better about who you were.

She is gone and that leaves a hole that we cannot fill in our lives

But may our sadness at our loss be consoled by the life she shared with us.

Lets not allow the bitterness of our parting to sour the sweetness, love and joy she brought into our lives.

Her footprints will be in and on our memories forever.

Thank you Peggy Ann for changing my life

May you find the peace that you so badly need.

RECOVERY

When trust has been broken it is hard to mend.

I had watched for several months as Peggy struggled without alcohol, minute by minute, hour by hour, day by day. Very slowly her health started to improve. Things remained frosty between us but we argued much less. She cooked the occasional meal, something we had learned to fear in the past as she was a danger to herself.

She had accepted that our marriage was over, that the house would be sold and she would live alone, possibly in a homeless unit. Still, she could learn to be independent again and maybe win back her self respect and that of her sons.

I wondered if there was a faint chance that the woman I had loved might find her way back. One evening, after work, I told her that I didn't know if we could ever trust each other or love each other again but if she wanted too and felt able, we could try. Peggy broke down with tears of pain, regret, guilt and relief, so did I.

From that point on we gave each other space and time to slowly rebuild all of those myriad connections that used to bind us together. Little by little we rediscovered why we had been together for so long. The love, respect and trust started to build.

Our sons, William and Mark, were and are delighted to have their parents back. They have been through a great deal and we are immensely proud of them both.

Peggy became more and more involved with a local addiction support group, she has made some amazing friends there and they have become very close. She also became much more engaged with her alcohol support councillor.

Our family life has improved beyond all recognition. We are not back to where we used to be, we are far better than that. Our near destruction as a family, and individually, has made us take a hard look at what is really important and what we value most. Our relationships are vital to our mental health and well-being. We no longer take them for granted.

We cannot change or forget what has happened to us but from the ashes of the old, we have a new life with a heightened sense of being alive, a greater appreciation of ourselves and others and a huge feeling of gratitude.

In September 2017, we participated in The Scottish Recovery Walk, in Dundee. It was a truly remarkable experience, to be part of almost two thousand people, proudly walking to celebrate the battles they had won and lost, the lives of those they had lost along the way, the fact that they were still in the game themselves, their shared humanity and the joy of striding along down the road to recovery.

MARK'S GIFT

A little while ago I wrote a poem for my son Mark. He was struggling with his studies and feeling frustrated because nothing seemed to help. Peggy and I are very proud of our boys and we know that we have put them through a great deal of pain and anxiety.

William and Mark are the most precious things in both of our lives. We are so grateful to have them in our lives. On this occasion Mark looked so lost and vulnerable. I just wanted to pick him up and carry him until he felt strong again. I thought if I wrote down how I felt, he could keep it and read it whenever he felt the need.

The words we write for our children are a legacy when we can't be there.

Although it was written with Mark in mind, I know he won't mind sharing its message with everyone. We all need to borrow someone else's light now and then.

MY GIFT

When you feel alone unloved unlovable
And so very unavailable and lost
Especially to yourself
Remember me

If I am permitted to give
But one gift
To you
I give you
Myself

It is all
I possess
And
All we may possess
And from that
Comes it's
Value

We spend our
Entire life
Becoming

But we begin our
Journey
With accepting

Acceptance of
Our self

Is the beginning
Of loving
Our self
And this we
Must do
In order to
Know love

When you learn
To love yourself
You
Light a beacon
That guides
Your way

You will grow
You will change
But always
You
Will
Shine

When the light
Is lost inside you
I give you
My light
Till
Yours
Shines through

And because
Acceptance
Is love
Please
Accept
My humble
Gift

STARS

We view our lives through the lens of relationship. We experience crippling pain and indescribable joy through and from our relationships.

We give and receive life enhancing gifts from one another, acceptance, recognition, empathy and love.

We are who we are because of our relationships or the lack of them. However, all of our relationships are shaped by and begin with our relationship with ourselves.

In order for me to find a way to accept, forgive and reconnect with my wife, Peggy, I needed to accept, forgive and reconnect with myself.

In my battle to save her and our family from her addiction, I lost my self. I tried to fight her fight for her and abandoned myself. Over time anger and resentment poisoned my connection to everyone and everything, including myself.

I blamed myself because I couldn't fix things and I wouldn't give up. Once I accepted that it wasn't my fight and withdrew, I started to heal.

I could not change or assume responsibility for Peggy's behaviour but I could and did change and be responsible for my own. As I became more comfortable in my own skin, my relationships with others improved.

When my journey back to self-respect and acceptance allowed, I recognised Peggy's journey too and how far she had come.

All through this we were carried along by amazing people. Without them we would not have made it. One special friend gave me a plaque with these words; "When you can't see ahead and it's too painful to look back, look beside you and there will be your friends".

We are all like stars, throughout our lives we shine and create light and warmth. The things we do, say or write touch others and sometimes light their way. Like stars we are lights in the darkness and the light we give outlasts our brief existence.

We all need to feel connected, accepted and valued. I hope that through these pages you have found new ways to connect, accept and value yourself and others.

We are all on life's journey, short or long and our common language is relationship.

AWAKENING

A poem for Peggy, to mark the beginning of our new life, on the road to recovery.

AWAKENING

At last
You have woken
From your
Nightmare

I didn't
Think
You ever
Would

I thought
My
Vigil over
And
Waited
Empty
For the
End

While you
Were
Gone
I
Searched
For myself
But
Found
Only shadows

Finally
I
Accepted my
New
Shrunken
Self
And
Looked ahead
Without
You

I turned
For one
Last
Look
Across
The void
Between
Us

I found
You
There
Beside me
Longing
Hoping
But
No longer
Lost

I reached
Out
Touched you
And
We both
Awoke
The nightmare
Retreating
The bonds
Of
Love
Returning

May we
Never
Lose
Our way
Again
Until
We
Close our
Eyes
For the final time

ORDINARY LIVES

We are connected to each other in a deep, felt and continuous line.

Stretching back through history to our parents, grandparents and beyond.

On to our partners' children and friends.

Into the future through grand children, great grand children, on and on.

Each of us have our own unique story and we touch each other's lives like drops of water in an ocean.

Every single one of us matters and is woven into the fabric of mankind.

There are no ordinary lives.

Printed in Great Britain
by Amazon